HOW A BILL BECOMES A LAW

BY KATHRYN WALTON

Please visit our website, www.enslow.com. For a free color catalog of all our high-quality books, call toll free 1-800-398-2504 or fax 1-877-980-4454.

Library of Congress Cataloging-in-Publication Data
Names: Walton, Kathryn, 1993- author.
Title: How a bill becomes a law / Kathryn Walton.
Description: Buffalo : Enslow Publishing, 2025. | Series: U.S. government
in review | Includes index.
Identifiers: LCCN 2023042321 | ISBN 9781978538054 (library binding) | ISBN
9781978538047 (paperback) | ISBN 9781978538061 (ebook)
Subjects: LCSH: Legislation–United States–Juvenile literature. | Bill
drafting–United States–Juvenile literature. | United States.
Congress–Juvenile literature.
Classification: LCC KF4945 .W35 2025 | DDC 328.73/077–dc23/eng/20231003
LC record available at https://lccn.loc.gov/2023042321

Published in 2025 by
Enslow Publishing
2544 Clinton Street
Buffalo, NY 14224

Copyright © 2025 Enslow Publishing

Portions of this work were originally authored by Kathleen Connors and published as *How Does a Bill Become a Law?* All new material in this edition is authored by Kathryn Walton.

Designer: Leslie Taylor
Editor: Natalie Humphrey

Photo credits: Cover (photo) create jobs 51/Shutterstock.com; series art (background) Apostrophe/Shutterstock.com; series art (stamp icon) Stocker_team/Shutterstock.com; p. 5 VectorMine/Shutterstock.com; p. 7 Salivanchuk Semen/Shutterstock.com; p. 9 mark reinstein/Shutterstock.com; p. 10 US House of Representatives, Office of the Clerk/https://commons.wikimedia.org/wiki/File:US_House_of_Representatives_hopper_and_desk.jpg; p. 11 Katherine Welles/Shutterstock.com; p. 13 Jimmy Panetta/https://commons.wikimedia.org/wiki/File:House_Budget_Committee_meeting_-_2020-01-15.jpg; p. 14 Scott J. Ferrell/LOC.gov; p. 15 U.S. House Photographers/https://commons.wikimedia.org/wiki/File:McGovern_Chairing_First_Rules_Committee_Hearing_of_116th_Congress.jpg; p. 17 New Africa/Shutterstock.com; p.18 HelloSSTK/Shutterstock.com; p. 19 ItzaVU/Shutterstock.com; p. 21 Dmitry Demidovich/Shutterstock.com; p. 23 Tada Images/Shutterstock.com; p. 25 Maxx-Studio/Shutterstock.com; p. 28 StockSmartStart/Shutterstock.com; p. 29 MDart10/Shutterstock.com.

All rights reserved. No part of this book may be reproduced in any form without permission in writing from the publisher, except by a reviewer.

Printed in the United States of America

Some of the images in this book illustrate individuals who are models. The depictions do not imply actual situations or events.

CPSIA compliance information: Batch #CSENS25: For further information, contact Enslow Publishing at 1-800-398-2504.

CONTENTS

Laws in the United States 4
The Beginning 6
Sponsoring a Bill 8
The Committees 12
The Mark-Up Session 16
Majority Rules 20
Passing in Both Houses 22
No Action 26
Steps to a Bill Becoming a Law 30
Glossary 31
For More Information 32
Index 32

Words in the glossary appear in **bold** the first time they are used in the text.

Laws in the United States

Laws are an important part of making our **society** run smoothly. Both everyday people and government bodies need to follow laws. In the U.S. government, the body that makes laws is called Congress. It gets its power from the U.S. **Constitution**!

The Constitution sets up three different branches of government. Each branch has different powers that make sure no one branch gets too powerful.

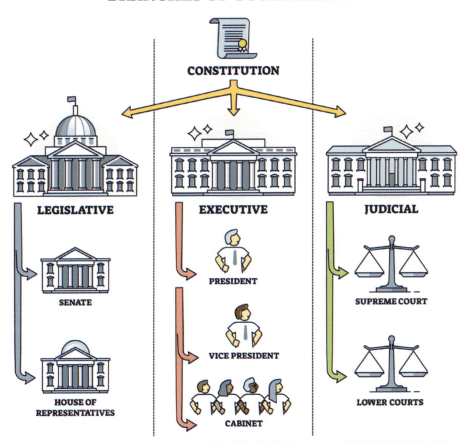

Legislative Branch
The body that makes laws. Made up of the Senate and the House of **Representatives**.

Executive Branch
The body that signs bills into law or **rejects** them. It is led by the president. It also includes the vice president and the president's **cabinet**.

Judicial Branch
The body that checks if laws follow the Constitution. Made up of the Supreme Court and the lower courts.

The Beginning

Laws start as bills. A bill is a draft, or early form, of a law presented by members of Congress to their house of Congress. Almost all bills can start in either the Senate or the House of Representatives. Some bills can only start in one or the other.

If a bill has to do with revenue, or money, it can only be started in the House of Representatives.

Sponsoring a Bill

Each bill presented to Congress has a sponsor. A sponsor is a person who speaks for the bill. When a member of Congress sponsors a bill, they look for others to cosponsor it. Cosponsors show that the bill is **supported**.

The Senate has two senators from each state and 100 senators total. There are 435 members of the House.

U.S. Congress in session

9

A bill is presented to the Senate or the House of Representatives once it has some support. In the House, the bill is placed in a wooden box called "the hopper." The bill is then given a number and is sent to a special **committee** that will **research** it.

the hopper

Some ideas for bills come from a representative or senator's constituents. Constituents are the people who members of Congress represent. Constituents may ask their members of Congress to support bills about fixing roads or other ways of making people's lives better!

The Committees

Both houses of Congress have special committees **focusing** on different subjects. These committees know a lot about their subject! The committee members study and talk about the bill. They make changes to the bill based on what they know.

Committees that focus on armed services, how communities are powered, and U.S. **connections** with other countries are found in both the House and the Senate.

13

The committees hold hearings when they are considering a bill. Committee members listen to people who support the bill and those who don't. They can make a better decision about the bill after hearing what people think on both sides.

Most committee hearings are open to the public. This means anyone can go to them and learn about the bills being proposed, or suggested.

The Mark-Up Session

After the hearings, committee members hold a "mark-up" session, or meeting. Members look at everything they've learned about the bill. They may ask for amendments, or changes, to a bill. Then, they vote to keep the changes or not.

Some changes made during a mark-up session are very small. Members may only change a word or sentence. Some bills have much bigger changes, like adding or cutting whole parts of the bill!

After the mark-up session, the bill is reported, or brought back, to the whole House or Senate. The whole house then **debates** the bill. More amendments to the bill may be voted on. Sometimes, bills are sent back to the committee!

> Committees can table, or stop, bills before they make it to the Senate or House for debate. Bills are sent back to the committee if a group wants to make big changes to the bill.

19

Majority Rules

A majority needs to agree on a bill for it to pass in the house of Congress where it was introduced. Members of the house may vote by saying "yea" or "nay" for "yes" or "no." Members of the House can cast their votes using an electronic voting system.

A majority is the bigger part of a group of people or things. In the House, the majority is 218 people. In the Senate, the majority is 51 people.

21

Passing in Both Houses

After a bill passes in one house, it is sent to the other house. The bill goes through the same steps it went through in the house where it started. The bill may be changed again before it's voted on in the second house.

LEARN MORE

If one house makes many changes to a bill before it is passed in that house, it goes back to a committee. This committee works to find out why the houses didn't agree on the same bill and figure out any problems.

When a bill has passed in both the House and the Senate, it goes to the president. The president can sign the bill to pass it into law. The bill can also be vetoed, or stopped from becoming a law.

When a bill is vetoed, it is sent back to Congress with notes about why it was vetoed. Congress can **bypass** the president's veto if two-thirds of members in both houses vote to approve it!

President Joe Biden

No Action

Sometimes, the president takes no action on a bill. If Congress is in session, the bill becomes a law without the president's approval after 10 days. If Congress isn't in session, the bill won't become a law after 10 days have passed.

If the president holds onto a bill until Congress isn't in session and doesn't sign it, it's called a pocket veto.

If the president does sign a bill, that bill becomes a law. But a law can still be **challenged** in court if people don't think it follows the U.S. Constitution. If the challenge makes it to the Supreme Court, the law may be ruled unconstitutional!

A law being unconstitutional means that it goes against the Constitution. Sometimes, the Supreme Court rules that only part of a law is unconstitutional! Laws that are unconstitutional are struck down.

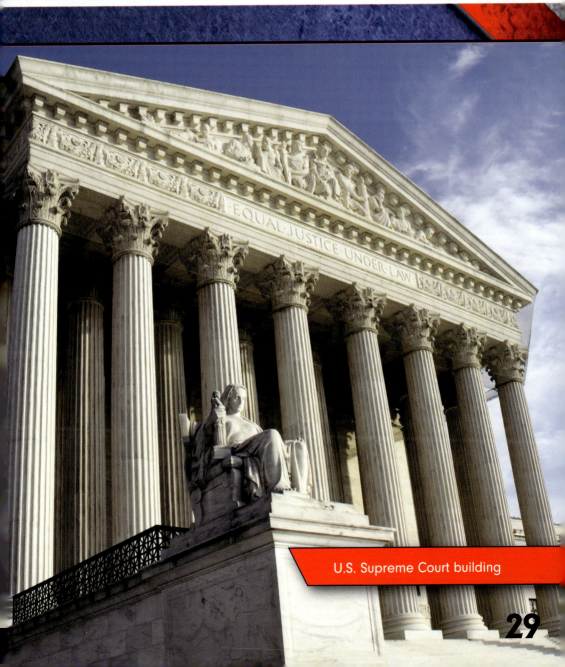

U.S. Supreme Court building

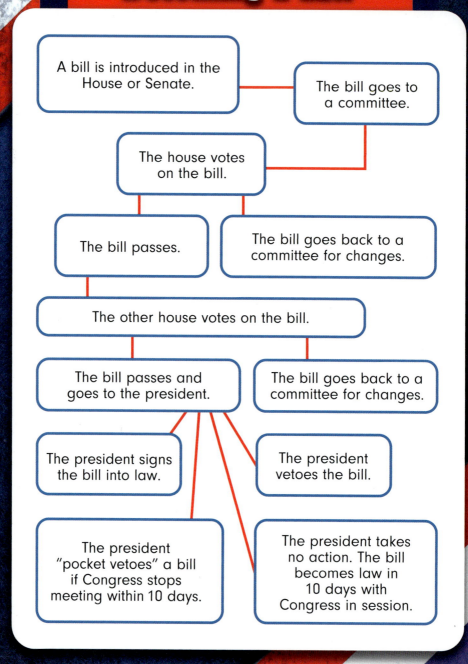

GLOSSARY

bypass: To circumvent, or get around, often using a clever strategy.

cabinet: A group of people who advise a government leader.

challenge: To say or show that something might not be legal, correct, or true.

committee: A small group that does a certain job.

connection: A relationship between people or groups who do business together.

constitution: The basic laws by which a country or state is governed.

debate: To argue a side. Also, an argument or public discussion.

focus: To have directed attention.

reject: To refuse.

representative: A member of a lawmaking body who acts for voters.

research: Studying to find something new.

society: The people who live together in an organized community with traditions, laws, and values.

support: To help or hold up.

For More Information

Books

Faust, Daniel R. *The Senate*. Minneapolis, MN: Bearport Publishing Company, 2022.

Rubinstein, Justine. *The House of Representatives*. Philadelphia, PA: Mason Crest, 2020.

Website

Kids in the House: How Does a Bill Become a Law?
https://kids-clerk.house.gov/grade-school/lesson.html?intID=17
Review more about how a bill becomes a law.

Publisher's note to educators and parents: Our editors have carefully reviewed this website to ensure that it is suitable for students. Many websites change frequently, however, and we cannot guarantee that a site's future contents will continue to meet our high standards of quality and educational value. Be advised that students should be closely supervised whenever they access the internet.

Index

amendments, 16, 18

branches of government, 5

Congress, 4, 6, 8, 10. 12, 20, 26, 30

constituents, 11

cosponsors, 8

hearings, 14, 16

House of Representatives, 5, 6, 7, 9, 10, 13, 18, 19, 21, 24, 30

money, 7

president, 5, 24, 26, 28, 30

Senate, 5, 6, 9, 10, 13, 18, 19, 21, 24, 30

sponsor, 8

Supreme Court, 5, 28, 29

table, 19

veto, 24, 27

vote, 16, 20, 24, 30